Bodies of Water

Rivers and Streams

Cassie Mayer

Heinemann Library
Chicago, Illinois

Customer Service 888-454-2279
Visit our website at www.heinemannraintree.com

Designed by Joanna Hinton-Malivoire
Photo research by Erica Martin
Printed and bound in China by South China Printing Co. Ltd.

12 11 10 09 08
10 9 8 7 6 5 4 3 2 1

ISBN-10: 1-4034-9364-2 (hc)
ISBN-10: 1-4034-9368-5 (pb)

The Library of Congress has cataloged the first edition of this book as follows:
Mayer, Cassie.
  Rivers and streams / Cassie Mayer.
    p. cm. -- (Bodies of water)
  Includes bibliographical references and index.
  ISBN-13: 978-1-4034-9364-4 (hc)
  ISBN-13: 978-1-4034-9368-2 (pb)
  1. Rivers--Juvenile literature. I. Title.
  GB1203.8.M39 2008
  551.48'3--dc22
                    2006034054

Acknowledgements
The publishers would like to thank the following for permission to reproduce photographs: Brand X Images pp. **8, 12**; Corbis pp. **4** (NASA), **17** (David Muench), **18** (B.S.P.I.), **19** (photocuisine/Gauter), **20** (Buddy Mays), **21** (Free Agents Limited), **23** (rice field: B.S.P.I.; cargo ship: Buddy Mays); Getty Images pp. **5** (Photonica/Bridget Webber), **6** (Iconica/David Zimmerman), **7** (LOOK/Florian Werner), **9** (The Image Bank/Preston Schlebusch), **11** (Purestock), **13** (George Kavanagh), **14** (Photodisc); Nature Picture Library p. **16** (Kim Taylor); Punchstock p. **10** (UpperCut Images); Robert Harding p. **15** (Travel Library).

Cover photograph reproduced with permission of Jupiter Images (Workbook Stock/David Collier). Back cover photograph reproduced with permission of Brand X Images.

Every effort has been made to contact copyright holders of any material reproduced in this book. Any omissions will be rectified in subsequent printings if notice is given to the publishers.

Contents

Rivers

water

Most of the Earth is covered by water.

river

Some of this water is in rivers.

A river is water that flows across land.

River water is not salty.

It is called fresh water.

Streams

A stream is a very small river.

Streams may run into rivers.

How Rivers Form

Rainwater runs down a mountain.

Rainwater forms streams.

Streams join together.
They make a river.

Rivers wash away soil.
Rivers wash away rock.

valley

Rivers can form valleys.

Where Rivers End

Some rivers flow into the ocean.

Some rivers flow into lakes.

River Life

Rivers have many animals.

Rivers have many plants.

How We Use Rivers

Farmers use rivers to water crops.

People use rivers for drinking water.

People use rivers to move goods.

People use rivers to see new places.

River Facts

The Nile is the longest river in the world. It is in Africa.

The Mississippi River is the largest river in North America.

Picture Glossary

crop a plant that is grown for something, such as food

goods things that people buy and sell

Index

Note to Parents and Teachers
This series introduces bodies of water and their unique characteristics. Discuss with children bodies of water they are already familiar with, pointing out bodies of water that exist in the area in which they live. You can use page 12 to introduce the concept of erosion and how water can change the shape of landforms.

The text has been chosen with the advice of a literacy expert to enable beginning readers success in reading independently or with moderate support. An expert in the field of geography was consulted to ensure accurate content. You can support children's nonfiction literacy skills by helping them use the table of contents, headings, picture glossary, and index.